ES

ESCAPE

STUCK IN MY HEAD

ANITA TEYISE

ESCAPE

CONTENTS

PREFACE

I sat reminiscing about all my brain activities and thoughts; I then decided to write a book and share it with you. My anxiety came crawling when I picked up a pen, and my thoughts vanished for a little while. They felt unsafe being shared in the real world. However, the point of this book is to reduce the hole I dug in my head slightly. This is a part of me, the unspoken part of me. I hope reading this book makes you feel better about your unspoken thoughts, just a tiny bit. I yearn to get out of this dark light. Walk with me.

Love: Anita

DEDICATION

To those who Love and
Not be loved

ESCAPE

SELF

ESCAPE

This is about me.

No one else but me!

ESCAPE

My skin shredded into small paper particles easily blown away by the wind. My brain smells like a microwave burnt foil filled with the exhaust of tossing and turning in one place

ESCAPE

I am a broken flask

My scars don't show to the
outside world.

ESCAPE

People will always know what you CHOOSE to tell them about you, yet they constantly try to use that kind of vulnerability as a weapon.

BULLIES!

I don't aspire to be understood by others. Consider that an expectation, which is forever accompanied by disappointment.

AWARENESS!

I am an imperfect person living
in a world that seeks perfection
from broken people.
Brokenness is labeled as a flaw
that needs to be hidden from the
face of the world.

FAKE!

I feel everything so deeply; I can be sensitive, I am careless at times, I'm very forgetful, I am humble, I am a multitasking person, I don't like humans sometimes, I am impulsive sometimes, I am vigilant, I am yielding.

SELF!

ESCAPE

See! the problem is not that I
don't know me
I know me but I want you to
know me too.

What if I am forever broken?

What if there is no fixing me?

SCARED!

I got so used to being second.
Now I'm making it a pattern by
NOT trusting people who put
me first.

DAMAGED!

ESCAPE

The worst feeling is walking on
these bumpy grains of the earth,
feeling completely dead inside.

Feeling yourself liquefying
while slowly evaporating as the
sun hits hard, destroying every
trace of me.

FADING

I am in extreme pain right now;
it's all emotional, I can feel my
chest sinking into a deep hole
and my heart burning up with
dreadful pain; I don't even
know why; I feel like
everything got collected into
one big fireball piercing through
my skin.

My soul is tired.

Silence! It speaks to my soul so loud that I finally discover myself, but then I hear some noise approaching.

My thoughts get twisted, and then I'm back to confusion. I like people around me, yes! But I'd love for them to quiet down and love me silently.

Ugh, silly me! I love assurance too, don't get me wrong, but I think I prefer silence, or am I used to it so much that I think of it as a preference?

ESCAPE

I lost her; now I'm looking for
her.

Seasonal chance might sound cliché, but quite honestly, it's reality.

Do not throw away the blanket before spring; you might freeze to death and miss out on the blooming flowers.

Hold on to the blanket.

KEEP WARM

ESCAPE

I was once a dying flower,
but now I bloom in fall.

I'm tearing myself apart, causing myself pain; I'm quite aware of it.

Pain is easier to obtain than love,

I took what came first.

Focusing more on yourself heals the soul; it helps the inner you. I guess that's why it is the hardest thing to do; it's time to find who you are. Sometimes you think you know, only to find out you had no idea of your capabilities, you can be a danger to yourself if you don't know who you are, and it's easy for people to crawl under your skin when you, yourself don't know anything about you.

Discover yourself and heal!

Now that you know me,
please allow me to share the
uncomfortable parts of me.

With anxiety creeping in as I
press my fingers against this
keyboard, thinking of all the
ways this could go wrong,
however, I have been stuck
in my head for so long.

ESCAPE

YOU

ESCAPE

ESCAPE

The one I gave a piece of me

YOU

Loving someone can be a
blessing and a curse, but you
sure were my curse but I think
it's okay that you are stuck in
my head with me, at least I'm
not sitting alone even though
your company is unpleasant. I
find the plate full of hurt more
filling than an empty plate.
Maybe you will decide to leave
as everyone did before, but I'll
sit here and consume the pain,
just until you get tired of using
me as a tool to fix something
that's missing within you.

I am a sunflower who enjoys
your honey and stings; I watch
my friends pick out the thorns
as you plan your next nest.

A CYCLE OF PAIN AND
SWEETNESS

You walked into my garden and picked me with my roots

Planted me in yours, now you forget to water me

I started to appreciate rainy days more than the rays of sunshine so that I could bloom again.

DISPLACED!

I always fall for things that don't belong to me.

Now I am paralyzed by the consequences.

SEQUENCE!

THE MIND TRAP

At first, I felt nothing for you!
You kept fishing for me

Once I was hooked, you let go
of the rod

Now I'm a drowning fish
hoping maybe someone will
unhook me from your mind
trap.

ESCAPE

I never had a face to fill my beautiful fantasies.

When you came into my life, it all made sense; my blanks were filled.

I wanted it to be you.

LONELINESS!

You came from behind. You blew my little bubble away

And shook the ground I was standing on.

I wonder what it's like to be loved by you.

CRAVING!

I know that you think you were protecting me.

I know that leaving was what's best according to you

I know you thought I was getting too attached.

I know you thought I wasn't yours, but what if you were wrong?

You left, and I felt exposed; I fell face down!

Just so you know, your leaving never protected me; it scared me.

I didn't mind you taking away
pieces of me,

I just enjoyed giving you
something that's mine.

With you, my words didn't
matter
My thoughts we never voiced
My tongue was tied
I said things I thought you
wanted to hear
I listened to you talk while
overthinking my response
Afraid you might leave when I
say the wrong things
Revisiting our conversations in
my head when you start
ignoring me.
A chest full of unspoken words
directed to you

#UNSEEN

I told you I would give you a
piece of me without a doubt
You laughed because it sounded
insane
Crazy because I meant all of it
I would cut off my skin to patch
your open scar
Cut off a finger to patch yours
I could give you my heart to
hold just so you could
physically feel my heartbeat.

ESCAPE

I was at a degree in my life
where I was numb to emotion

I felt pity for no one until
something bad happened to you.

YOU MADE ME FEEL AGAIN!

His voice is like a melody; his laugh massages my heart; with him around, I feel complete. Something about him completes me; I still wonder what it is because treating me right is not it.

The moment you didn't want me, I KNEW! But I still wanted you, so I stayed.

Fear of not being wanted.

ESCAPE

I didn't stop caring about you; I just stopped showing it. No matter how hard I tried, you just wouldn't get it.

INVISIBLE!

I don't even want ample from you. All I craved was to be yours. My anxiety takes over me most of the time but somehow, talking to you quiets my world. I know it's strange and might be too much for you, but I promise, to date you is the last thing I want now. I know we are not good as lovers but rather perfect as friends. There's an incentive why you liked me once, and I'd love to know why, but that doesn't matter now because what I want to know now is why? Why is it so easy for people to leave me? Why was it so easy for you to walk away from me and not even miss me for a second?

Maybe I'm never going to know because maybe I'd never even speak to you again, but I hope you find happiness. Bouncing around numerous people and behaving like you don't care is miserable. It's time to believe that someone can like you for you, and there's nothing more to it. I don't know what was so different about YOU, but this is the first and last time I'd ever assemble to someone who was absolutely nothing to me like I did you. You treated me like garbage, but I guess it was all necessary for growth. I'll forever love you ♥

ESCAPE

You were the perfect fantasy
my story has been looking for;
you fit in so perfectly in my
counterfeit.

With you it was never about intimacy.

It was about how you made me feel without having to physically touch me.

The state of Flux

In this relationship, you placed me precariously, yet here I am sitting so comfortably.

DENIAL!

Yesterday I woke up thinking about how I wish we never met.

Today I wish I'd meet you all over again.

UNCERTAINTY!

ESCAPE

You only asked for my
nakedness; I confused it with
love.

MY FAULT!

I keep telling myself I don't have to stop loving you to let you go; however, the void of pain hurts me more instead.

I MISS YOU HURTING ME!

ESCAPE

I thought saying no to him would make him leave, but when he was done with me, he left anyway.

DON'T SELL YOURSELF SHORT!

My friends watch me lie to them, to me, to my feelings, about being over you

While they all nod in silence.

FRIENDSHIP!

I miss you today, and every other day, so I decided to start this folder just so I can feel like I'm talking to you.

You are not mine; you were never mine!
I don't want you to be mine, but I do.

I want you to call me like you used to. I want us to talk! I don't want to be your friend, really, but I don't want to be your lover; I just want YOU! To talk to you, that's all.

CONFUSED!

Isn't it insane that you can feel this way about a person? Because for me, it is!

The craziest thing, we've never dated, but I'd choose you over any man I've ever met.

ALLUSION!

I never want to not talk to you, ever! Crazy, right?

HYPNOTIZED!

The first time twenty-four hours went by without your tone beeping on my phone, I knew it was happening again.

DESERTION!

ESCAPE

I want you to date other
people and be happy, I
promise but always talk to
me! Until I know how to let
go of you.

STUCK!

ESCAPE

You would never understand
the pain you caused me, and I
don't want you to because
I'm the one who felt it, and I
know it's not all on you! It's
on me, too, because I allowed
all of it. You didn't try for
anything, but I gave you
everything.

WHY?

I was hoping you would have called me by now to check on me just so I'd know you are thinking of me. But you couldn't even call me on my birthday. I was never really anything to you, and yet here

I thought you were my destination, but you were just yet another life lesson.

DESPERATION!

ESCAPE

I called you today, and you know what's funny? I knew you won't return that call. I needed you this time, or I wouldn't have called; it's okay; I'm not mad at you; I'm just done with you.

HOPE!

I'm so sorry I used you as a shield when I broke my own heart by clinging to you; you played me, yes! But you didn't hide that I was just an instrument you enjoyed momentarily. I just got so attached to the beautiful melody, forgetting that you act shitty sometimes.

STRINGS!

Today I admitted to myself that I could let you go if I wanted, but I realized I just don't want to yet.

That made everything hurt less because all I want is you to consider me as a person. Something in you weirdly completes me, so yeah; I'll be sticking around for a moment.

DELUSIONAL!

The dreams about you are never-ending; my brain is running all night, creating beautiful stories that would never be real. So, it's my brain that doesn't want to let go. I don't feel like talking to you anymore for now.

FANTASY!

My heart doesn't miss you anymore :(that makes me so sad.

ACCEPTANCE!

I didn't let go of you because I wanted to!

I had to understand you do not prison people into your life, calling it love.

As much as I wanted you, you didn't!

So, I set you free of me.

LETTING GO!

Dreams used to be a waterfall of honey

Now it all turned into a thorny nightmare.

BEE!

The last time I saw you, is the last memory I have of you. I pressed pause, and I refused to press play.

ESCAPE

I lost my heart in a fight of love
But this is not about you
Let's turn the page.

CLEAN SLATE!

ARBITRARY

Can someone remind me what happiness tastes like? How does it smell? What does it look like? Or maybe how it feels like? I just feel like I'm not alive; tell me, is it possible to feel like there's no air while you walk outside, feel trapped, but you don't know where and how. I don't know how to explain the feeling. It confuses me sometimes. Tell me! Is it possible to not know what your heart desires anymore? My brain feels like some flaky ice, my body like a trembling stone, and my head so heavy. All I want now is to remember how happiness was defined.

Why are you crying? "You asked" I don't know; tears flow through when I have excessive thoughts; I can't share with anyone, not even myself, since my brain is scorching. When did it get to this? I know there's a better way out of this self-annihilation. To be honest, I hate crying; all I want to do is yell so blare I just never get the time to do it.

Suicidal thoughts are not my cup of weight, but I mostly feel like hurting myself just to feel physical pain, maybe for a little while I'll forget about the emotional and spiritual affliction.

Do you think they will cry when I die? Why would they be crying? No one knows how I'm doing, but I know how everyone is doing, so why would they cry? Will they be thinking about who will listen to their problems now? But remember nobody asked how I was doing? All I know is, "hi, how are you" obviously, I say I'm good; that is the reply everyone is expecting, right? "I'm good," huh, and you know what I say to them. "How are you feeling?" Or "How did everything go" not that I'm expecting them to return the shoulder, but all I'm saying is, Will they cry? Why would they be crying?

For a moment, I did smell it; it's like mint blowing through your nose; did I tell you? I also heard it; it sounds like a heavy wind. What does that even imply? Was it there to take me with it forever, or was it just giving me a taste of how amazing it would be to have it forever? I was just wondering, ow yeah, you say I worry too much; do you want to trade stands for a day? Experience being me just a day? I'm sure not. I also wouldn't want to trade with someone else, but I'd love to trade with myself. I just can't get over how it really smells like *Sigh*. Ow! What am I talking about? HAPPINESS.

Get to know it; it needs you to spend more time figuring it out; it's not easy to find. It all takes time; you must look for it within sometimes; it doesn't even stay long; you feel it today, then the next day you just feel void. Therefore, you shouldn't force it so that when you find it, it will all feel real. I know I told you about how it smells, and I still smell it. Hopefully, I'll feel it soon. I can't wait to just feel all the physical, emotional, and mental touch of it; if the scent does so much within, I just wonder what the touch might do.

HAPPINESS! I sometimes ask myself, is love really what everyone wants? Or do we all think we want it because no one knows what it feels like? Maybe we all have it; maybe no one has ever experienced it. You never know what love is; I just think it's possible that it just doesn't exist at all. In my world, I always give what I think love is, or maybe I think I do, but how come no one does the same, they say they love you, yes, but it all feels like LUST or LIKE not to <u>LOVE</u>. I don't know if I can compare Love and Happiness, maybe not! Because happiness does exist, it's just hard to find. Do you think love might be like that too? I keep on wondering.

ESCAPE

Are you asking me why I don't tell anyone? Do you know the real world? Tell anyone, huh! These are the words they use to those who do... Dramatic, Attention seeker, Overreacting, sensitive, and more, which maybe some of the labels are true, but that doesn't mean I don't want to be heard? we are all created differently, being the reason why we suffer loneliness in different ways, and we try to protect our feelings differently. Therefore, I believe no one will understand now because I can't even explain it myself; I don't know what I'm feeling; I just feel empty and heavy inside. How do I tell anyone that? How

do I explain? Who will
understand without judgment?

Fear? Killer of success. Guess what! I feel it almost every day; when I think about being in a relationship, my heart starts racing; I just feel it suffocating; it must be fear, right? How does one help it? How do I press pause? I'm even scared of thinking. I feel these heavy chains on my shoulders, and they are making a lot of noise; I feel like running fast, but my legs are not moving; I want to scream so bad; the voice is not coming out. What kind of life is this? It's draining every fiber of my bones; I just want to think without fear of consequence.

It's funny how your life can spin around in 24 hours, 1440 minutes, and 86400 seconds. Decisions change, and uncertainty occurs. I wake up knowing who I am, yet I always go to bed filled with doubt and confusion

24 hours can make or break

Doubt! I know what you are going to say; I'm just a troubled girl. The question is what troubles me? Doubting myself, every move I make, even when I speak, I feel like I'm saying the wrong things; I listen to my voice and think, is this how a human being should even sound? That's absurd, right? There are days when I love myself so much: my heart is full of self-acceptance, but it just all goes away in a blink of an eye. How do I hold on to the feeling forever?

Maybe I am a troubled girl that no one likes, maybe not; maybe I'm just uniquely different from the world that it might take time for it to understand me. It all goes back to doubt and fear

Do you think nature responds to humankind? Because I feel like it does. It says a lot of things to me, some I don't understand yet, but some I do. Do you think the wind just blows for no reason? Leaves fall while some remain on trees. Is the grass green but parched on the other side? I sometimes think we just keep on surviving without understanding things or people we survive with. Have you ever thought about how amazing birds are? The sound they make might mean something; don't you think? Have you ever tried talking to the sun? Do you know how beautiful it is when it responds?

NATURE!

Why do people always torture themselves with envy? Hatred does your soul no good; it's poison in your system, controlling your thoughts, and you just turn into a robot of hate. When will it ever stop? Do you ask yourself that? Hating someone who doesn't even think about you, yet they get to have a peaceful night every day. You! on the other hand, all you do is rot your life. Make peace and move on. Don't invest in hate so much that you end up hating and hurting yourself unknowingly.

FORGIVENESS!

ESCAPE

I'm just a sunflower surrounded
by roses, but they turn to forget
I bloom too.

An ear to listen to! Do they even know what that means? If someone is inadequate to listen, then you mention a shoulder to cry on. Do you think that can be possible? We are born in a world full of narcissistic behavior.

I listen to myself, I advise myself, I offer myself a shoulder to cry on, I complain only to myself, but there are times where I feel myself leaving me, a point where I find it hard to catch my breath, but in it all, I know better days always come, and I'm not the only one, it's not the end of the world right? People do care a little, right? At least my family still wants me alive, right?

Sometimes the hardest thing in life is yourself. We always judge ourselves before anyone does; why? Why are we so hard on ourselves? Why can't we just appreciate who we are and who we are becoming? It's sad when you always seek approval from people who never give it to you because you always think you are not good enough.

SELF SABOTAGE!

It's hard when people love you when their first choices disappoint them. I'm just wondering why I am always people's side wall; how does one remove a caring heart?

OPTION!

ESCAPE

Sometimes it is okay to just flip the page.

ESCAPE

LOSS

I miss loving someone
effortlessly.

I miss saying those four-letter
words without them slicing
through my heart.

Most of all, I miss hearing those
words and believing them

I miss feeling loved.

VOID!

Hey, can I ask something?
When people die, how do you
know that they are okay, or they
are in a good place? Do you
think they really hear us when
we talk to them? No! I'm just
wondering if they even
remember who we are. Do they
miss us? Why did they leave?
Do they even care how we feel?
Does it hurt the same way with
them too, or are they really at
peace? This means they don't
miss us! Do you think they had
a choice to live or die? Maybe
because of the beauty on the
other side, they decided to let
go? I just wonder why someone
would leave you in such pain...

ESCAPE

I thought it was okay to move
on after losing you, but every
time someone hurts me, I think
of how happy I could have been
if you were still here.

GRIEF!

I cannot write about losing you
I don't want to ponder the
emotion
You still live in my heart
The thought of feeling your loss
will destroy me
7 years later that is a pain I'm
not ready to feel

ESCAPE

3 am is not my favorite hour

I lost you in the dawn of July.

You left me with the greatest gift.

But never prepared me on how to assemble it without you.

MOTHERHOOD!

ESCAPE

When you are a mother, you don't get to the breakdown; you don't press pause.

You keep moving for your seed to grow in a healthy soil.

PARENTING!

ESCAPE

Dear child, I'm sorry that you
must experience this wicked
world as a fatherless child.

LOSS!

ESCAPE

Appreciate people leaving you
without being mad at them.

THE LIVING!

Dear friend

You were sent into my life as a directing angel, but now we are falling apart; it's best we let go before we crash.

ACCEPTANCE!

Just because someone helped you through a circumstance in life doesn't mean you should be stuck with them forever. Let them go and be forever thankful they crossed your path.

GROWTH!

Why do we lose friends? The ones we think are our forever. Do you ever wonder if they think of us too sometimes? I ask myself every day; I feel like it's possible they only think of us as people they used to know or some trivia... Psssh, I don't know.

UNSOLVED!

Is it possible to miss someone so much if you haven't seen them in Years? When you still hear their voices like you just heard them yesterday, still remember what they looked like when you last saw them? Their smell and how warm the hug was, long chats, lilting laughter, and all the food you shared.

MEMORIES!

"Once upon a time" doesn't mean forever; just appreciate the fact that someone was once in your life. Don't force the past into the present because you won't obtain a great future... today to all my "once upon a time," I'm letting go. I'm glad you were once present in my life.

I couldn't think about losing any longer; I had to find a replacement for grief.

DENIAL!

HOPE

Here we are

Open to

Pain if

Everyone thinks we are happy

We make hope an image instead
of believing in the beauty of
things.

Hope can mend or destroy you.

We keep holding on to bad situations hoping things will change

Truth is they might or might not, or by the time they change, you'd be too broken to mend

We hold on to ropes that cut through our hands, ripping our veins apart with no mercy, yet we excuse all that with hope.

ESCAPE

The random phone calls

Social media reactions

Random text messages

Giving delusive contentment

Saying all those beautiful things
just to keep me in your dungeon

I need you to drop this case

I'm tired of enjoying being your
prisoner

You might open these gates to
let me out, and I might still stay
here

Do not come back to check if I
left or not; that would delay me
into thinking you still care.

FALSE HOPE!

I must trust the rain as it leaves traces on my skin

walking down this dark empty street, feeling every drop in my face and my heart filled with the hope of beautiful things because that is what happens when you trust the rain, your brain blooms with beautiful flowers.

This ride is making me car sick,
or should I say lovesick.
The motion is just not pleasant.
We move in slow motion, then
fast and wavy, and suddenly
stop in the middle of a busy
highway. Cars pass by, some
yielding to check on me, but
I'm too caught up in the stuck
car to notice the help being
offered.

When I started to look up, my
anxiety couldn't handle the
sight of crossing the road
without; you started moving
again.

I'm sick of the never-ending
breakdowns, I hope you find a
good parking spot

I want to get off!!!!

CLOSURE

ESCAPE

I saw you fall in love with
someone else right in front of
me

You forced me to closure when
I still had the door wide open
for you

I was prepared to mend the
brokenness while you collected
all my broken pieces and put
them in a trash can

I guess it was all your closure
but never mine.

DUMPED!!!

ESCAPE

I felt all my real-life pain
without pinning it on you.

I cannot use the pain you caused
as a shield to every unfortunate
encounter.

CAMOUFLAGE!

ESCAPE

I thought the love I imagined
was what made me stay in bad
situations

Until I found true love and
realized, I found comfort in pain

I stayed because the pain made
me feel again

When there was no love and
care, pain showed up for me
and gave me a home

Pain gave me closure

ESCAPE

I stepped out of the fantasy
world.

I no longer needed him to
recognize me.

HEALING!

The silence brings realization
When It's just me and my
thoughts
The time where reality reflects
The truth settles in
It was never a story about two
people
It's a story about one who tried
for what failed

I feel more alive now because I believe dead flowers can bloom again too, everything is seasonal like leaves fall in autumn and bloom again in spring. Don't be a tree that dies in winter, have hope for spring so you can experience summer.

Take walks

Feel the air damp in your skin, hear the birds chirping, hear the water running through stones. Lay outside on the grass and look up the blue sky, enjoy the clouds and silence. Forget about all else and enjoy the sound of peace. Imagine the beauty of the world happening within you, because you are part of nature and nature reacts to seasonal change

You made them feel special
Your love painted them colorful
Take that away and you'll
realize how ordinary they are.
Pack up your crayons and leave
that page black and white

PORTRAIT

Facing reality is understanding
that the only closure you need is
acceptance

ESCAPE

ESCAPE

Never give up on love
Love and love loud
Allow yourself to feel the pain
Just so you can allow yourself to love again
Love is a blessing don't curse it
Keep watering your self so you can bloom in
the dark.

Made in the USA
Middletown, DE
10 November 2022

14440811R00073